Orchard and Vineyard

Orchard and Vineyard

V. Sackville-West

MINT EDITIONS

Orchard and Vineyard was first published in 1921.

This edition published by Mint Editions 2021.

ISBN 9781513212203 | E-ISBN 9781513212104

Published by Mint Editions®

MINT EDITIONS

minteditionbooks.com

Publishing Director: Jennifer Newens
Design & Production: Rachel Lopez Metzger
Project Manager: Micaela Clark
Typesetting: Westchester Publishing Services

Contents

Songs of Fancy

Sailing

HUMANITIES

Mariana in the North

All her youth is gone, her beautiful youth outworn,
Daughter of tarn and tor, the moors that were once her home
No longer know her step on the upland tracks forlorn
    Where she was wont to roam.

All her hounds are dead, her beautiful hounds are dead,
That paced beside the hoofs of her high and nimble horse,
Or streaked in lean pursuit of the tawny hare that fled
    Out of the yellow gorse.

All her lovers have passed, her beautiful lovers have passed,
The young and eager men that fought for her arrogant hand,
And the only voice which endures to mourn for her at the last
    Is the voice of the lonely land.

Sorrow of Departure

For D.

He sat among the shadows lost,
And heard the careless voice speak on
Of life when he was gone from home,
Of days that he had made his own,
Familiar schemes that he had known,
And dates that he had cherished most
As star-points in the year to come,
And he was suddenly alone,
Thinking (not bitterly,
But with a grave regret) that he
Was in that room a ghost.

He sat among the shades apart,
The careless voice he scarcely heard.
In that arrested hour there stirred
Shy birds of beauty in his heart.

The clouds of March he would not see
Across the sky race royally,
Nor yet the drift of daffodil
He planted with so glad a hand,
Nor yet the loveliness he planned
For summer's sequence to fulfil,
Nor trace upon the hill
The annual waking of the land,
Nor meditative stand
To watch the turning of the mill.

He would not pause above the Weald
With twilight falling dim,
And mark the chequer-board of field,
The water gleaming like a shield,
The oast-house in the elms concealed,
Nor see, from heaven's chalice-rim,

The vintaged sunset brim,
Nor yet the high, suspended star
Hanging eternally afar.

These things would be, but not for him.

At summer noon he would not lie
One with his cutter's rise and dip,
Free with the wind and sea and sky,
And watch the dappled waves go by,
The sea-gulls scream and slip;
White sails, white birds, white clouds, white foam,
White cliffs that curled the love of home
Around him like a whip. . .
He would not see that summer noon
Fade into dusk from light,
While he on shifting waters bright
Sailed idly on, beneath the moon
Climbing the dome of night.

This was his dream of happy things
That he had loved through many springs,
And never more might know.
But man must pass the shrouded gate
Companioned by his secret fate,
And he must lonely go,
And none can help or understand,
For other men may touch his hand,
But none the soul below.

Scorn

They roll, clan by clan, kin by kin, on wide orderly roads,
Burghers and citizens all, in a stately procession,
Driving before them the wealth of their worldly possession,
Cattle, and horses, and pack-mules with sumptuous loads.

In velvet and fur and fat pearls,—rich lustre and sheen,
Paunches and plenty, and fatuous voices contented
Counting their gain, and their women all jewelled and scented
Smiling false smiles with the little sharp word in between.

But those in the by-paths of vagrancy, star-gazers, they,
Ragged and feckless and young, with no thought but their singing,
Derisive of gain, and light as the bird in its winging,
Stopping to kiss or to frolic, the simple and gay,

God's fools,—the belovèd of God who made them and the wind,
Gipsies and wastrels of life, the heedless of warning,
Chasing the butterfly now on the breeze of the morning,
Laugh at the passing procession that leaves them behind.

V. SACKVILLE-WEST

DISSONANCE

Clamour has riven us, clamour and din.
My hand reaches blindly out for your hand, but within
My mind cannot reach to your mind, because of the clamour and din.

Clang as of brass, an uproar that will not cease.
I would take from the strangest god or devil the gift of peace.
If the strife that divides us were suddenly stilled and would cease

I could come to you, come under washed void skies,
My thought in your thought embraced, my eyes and your eyes
Levelly meeting without the quick faltering of disguise.

But all is a harshness and rack where in vain
We strive through the grossness of flesh to discover our souls again,
And the closer we clasp one another, the further apart remain.

On the Statue of a Vestal Virgin
by Toma Rosandić

How slender, simple, shy, divinely chaste,
She wilting stood,
Her suppleness at pause, by leisure graced,
In robes archaic by the chisel woo'd,
That smoothly flowed around her waist
And all her figure traced,
And at her feet in fluid ripples broke;
A Vestal virgin! but she rather seemed
The Hamadryad of the sculpted oak
Since in that oaken raiment she for ever dreamed.

One finger to her lips she raised,
And turned her dubious glances wide
As one who forward to the future gazed,
But her reluctant body swerved away
As one who held her bounty back with pride.
"Forbear!" her hesitation seemed to say,
While her exulting soul for instant capture cried.

And she was ageless; leisure unperturbed
Lay like a light across her brow
And sanctified her vow;
But that uplifted hand from its austerity
Another spirit stirred,
Spirit of grace, spirit of fantasy,
The wayward spirit of the pagan tree.

Had she stood dreaming by the water's verge,
Her branches mirrored in the forest pool
Where plashing sunlight flickered and was cool?
Did she so stand
Before the sculptor with his mortal hand
Summoned the mortal maiden to emerge?
And did she open eyes upon a place
All pied and jewelled with the flowers wild,

With king-cups and the pretty daisy mild,
With periwinkle sulking like a child,
And little orchis with his puckered face,
And campion too?
Did these, when first they saw her, race
Around her feet like tiny rivulets?
The bluebells shake for joy? the violets,
Thinking that other Virgin full of grace
Was come amongst them, blush a deeper blue?

Was this her birth upon a world of men,
Where any painter might have seized his hour,
Breathing her swiftly on the canvas then,
Among the lowly flowers a taller flower?
Or any sculptor on the marble limn
Her slenderness serene, her beauty's dower,
Her lifted hand, her smooth and fragile limb,
Learning a greater art from her than she from him?

So in the prison of her perfect shape
She dwelt for ever virginal, adored,
Whence she might never know escape,
Might never know what mystery lay stored
Beyond the threshold she might never pass,
But where for ever poised and wavering she was,
Threshold of waking youth, as bright and narrow as a sword.

TRIO

So well she knew them both! yet as she came
Into the room, and heard their speech
Of tragic meshes knotted with her name,
And saw them, foes, but meeting each with each
Closer than friends, souls bared through enmity,
Beneath their startled gaze she thought that she
Broke as the stranger on their conference,
And left them as she stole abashed from thence.

ARIANE

I wish you thought me faithless, when within
My heart I knew my innocence from sin.

I wish that I might tell you fables blithe
Of my misdeeds, and smile to see you writhe.

This I could bear; I cannot bear that you
Should think me faithful, when I am untrue.

BEFORE AND AFTER

Before

I wait your coming as a miracle,
And the expectant morning waits with me;
Time hangs suspended as a quiet bell
That once did strike the hours successively,
For over all the country lies a spell,
A hush, a painted stillness, where I see
(As calm as skies reflected in a well)
The fields enchanted, waiting silently.

After

Oh, heart! the beauty of your wind-swept hair
Blown from your temples as you swiftly came!
For all the pagan grace of you was there,
Remembered, ardent, after months the same.
The eager muscles of your throat were bare,
The candid passion lit you like a flame,
As, striving on against the countering air,
You reached me, failing, breathing out my name.

IRRUPTION

Well-greaved Achaians; lordliest Atreides;
Great-hearted friendship, foes no lesser-hearted;
Murmur of leaves on distant Latmos; coo
Of doves on Thisbe; pasture-land of horses,
Argos! and thou, the windy-beached Enispe;
Achaian fleet on that unvintaged sea,
Vessels of bronze and scarlet, beaked with gold,
In great procession Troy-wards, ranging wide
Over wide waters, bearing mighty captains,
Sons of the gods, the fosterlings of Zeus,
Casters of spear and javelin, fleet-footed
Or wise in council, flowing-haired Achaians,
—This was my epic and my company.

For you, Tintagel pinnacled on rocks
Emerged from desolate chords, until your mood
Wearied of saga; melted to the dusk
Falling on Spanish cities, when the shutters
Open again on evening, and the flute
Of some stray passing goat-herd down the street
Pipes idly, or the strident gay guitar
Befriends the lover's whisper at the window;
For you sat playing, and your fingers roamed
To Russia, where the simple is the blessed,
And woke both melancholy pomp and folly,
And passed again to fantasy that is
Homeless, and shies away from thoughts of home.
I read; you played; we had no need of speech.

They came, noisy and shrill, well-meaning; they
Spoke to us first of wealth and then of love,
The love of others, negligently shrewd
And empty in their chatter. Then they spoke,
Wise and judicious, and we answered them,

Judicious likewise, flattering their mood.
But our eyes found each other, and we fell
Suddenly silent, caught in treachery,
Remembering that proud world wherein we dwelt erstwhile.

To Eve

Because I knew you fickle as the flame
And sweet as music irresponsible,
    Because I knew no walls could tame
Your vagrancy within their certain shell,

I raised for you a palace on a hill
Where all the spirits generous and free
    Might drift at their unchidden will,
Or tarry to salute you carelessly.

A windy palace most fantastical,
Whose halls stood full of light and resonance,
    Where slender fountains lyrical
Spilled water like a stream of bright romance,

And, high above the many spires, I hung
A company of bells; with wanton hands
    The happy wind shook out and swung
Their dimpling music over level lands.

MAD

"I'll take my yellow neckerchief,
  My coral beads I'll wear;
  Green ivy-chains shall loop my dress,
  And ivy-chains shall loop my hair.

"What pretty gyves, such pretty gyves!
  See how with tendril twists
  They twine a halter round my throat
  And make soft captives of my wrists.

"I'll leave my shoes beside the stream,
  And creep on noiseless feet
  Between the willows all among
  The iris and the meadow-sweet."

  She slips from willow-tree to tree,
  Holding one finger pressed
  Against her lips; her other hand
  Lies lightly moulded on her breast,

  And peeping, laughing all the day,
  She rambles up and down,
  But I, unseen, have seen her go
  With ivy slung about her gown.

V. SACKVILLE-WEST

Escape

Come, shall we go, my comrade, from this den
Where falsehood reigns and we have dallied long?
Exchange the curious vanities of men
For roads of freedom and for ships of song?

We came as strangers, came to learn and look,
To hear their music, drink the wine they gave.
Now let us hence again; the happy brook
Shall quench our thirst, our music be the wave.

Come! they are feasting, let us steal away.
Beyond the doors the night awaits us, sweet.
Tomorrow we shall see the break of day,
And goat-herds' pipes shall lead our roaming feet.

To Eve in Tears

You laughed, and all the fountains of the East
Leapt up to Heaven with their diamond rain
To hang in light, and when your laughter ceased
Dropped shivered arrows to the ground again.

You laughed, and from the belfries of the earth
The music rippled like a shaken pool;
And listless banners at the breeze of mirth
Were stirred in harbours suddenly made cool.

You wept, and all the music of the air
—As when a hand is laid upon a bell—
Was stilled, and Dryads of the tossing hair
Crept back abashed within the secret dell.

Bitterness

Yes, they were kind exceedingly; most mild
Even in indignation, taking by the hand
One that obeyed them mutely, as a child
Submissive to a law he does not understand.

They would not blame the sins his passion wrought.
No, they were tolerant and Christian, saying, "We
Only deplore. . ." saying they only sought
To help him, strengthen him, to show him love; but he

Following them with unrecalcitrant tread,
Quiet, towards their town of kind captivities,
Having slain rebellion, ever turned his head
Over his shoulder, seeking still with his poor eyes

Her motionless figure on the road. The song
Rang still between them, vibrant bell to answering bell,
Full of young glory as a bugle; strong;
Still brave; now breaking like a sea-bird's cry "Farewell!"

And they, they whispered kindly to him "Come!
Now we have rescued you. Let your heart heal. Forget!
She was your danger and your evil spirit." Dumb,
He listened, and they thought him acquiescent. Yet,
(Knowing the while that they were very kind)
Remembrance clamoured in him: "She was wild and free,
Magnificent in giving; she was blind
To gain or loss, and, loving, loved but me,—but me!

"Valiant she was, and comradely, and bold;
High-mettled; all her thoughts a challenge, like gay ships
Adventurous, with treasure in the hold.
I met her with the lesson put into my lips,

"Spoke reason to her, and she bowed her head,
Having no argument, and giving up the strife.

She said I should be free. I think she said
That, for the asking, she would give me all her life."

And still they led him onwards, and he still
Looked back towards her standing there; and they, content,
Cheered him and praised him that he did their will.
The gradual distance hid them, and she turned, and went.

A Fallen Soldier

Hope held his hand and ran with him together.
Despair, the coward, at their coming fled.
Like a young ram, he shook his hornèd head,
And broke away from his restraining tether.
He loved the sea, he loved the cleansing flame;
No woman yet, his heart was all too young;
Over the plain of life his heart was flung,
Seeking for jeopardies that he might tame.
He cloaked his faith with laughter, but his faith
Was certain, as his confidence was gay,
And laughing went he, till on his last day
His hands stretched out to life were clasped by death.

Fallen Youth

O redolent things most dear to Youth on earth,
Friendship of other men; the hunter's horn;
The strong fatigue of practised limbs; the mirth
Of little birds in coppices and corn;
Work's satisfaction; leisure's bland delight;
The grateful sinking into sleep at night;

Speed, with the winds of heaven at your heels,
And grimy Power, and all you brilliant ones
That leap and sparkle 'mid the din of wheels,
A thousand little stars and little suns;
And streets of cities threatening the sky;
Cranes, wharves, and smoke in billows hanging high;

O stately Bridge, the country's arching frame,
A needle's eye to thread the river through;
Free ships, that rove and perish without fame;
Rich days of idleness, and soul that grew
Suddenly certain after doubting years,
And won through joy the wisdom lost through tears;

O Downs of Sussex, flowing swift and clean
Like stretchèd dogs along the English shore,
With cleanliness of athletes, and the lean
Brown flanks that course above the hare-belled floor;
O winds, that jangle all those little bells,
And tangle hair of nymphs in hidden dells;

O wandering Road, stranger and instant friend,—
For Youth a gipsy ever was at heart,—
Highway and packway, path with many a bend
That keep your mystery a thing of art;
O pools of friendly water; little lins;
O sudden views of country; wayside inns;

Labour of harvest; cider sweet and good;
Casual friends with tales of travel far;
Beauty of women; sunlight through a wood;
Companionable beasts; all things which are,
Weep for him! weep for Youth that laughed so bright,
Extravagantly fallen in the fight.

INSURRECTION

INSURRECTION

To A.

I

Poor soul! a captive in a prison-house
Dreaming of pastures, is not more degraded
Through rags and shackles and the insidious louse,
And naked splendour of the body faded,

Than our uneasy spirit, dimly haunted
By vision of some state, some wisdom whole;
Prophetic down unhoped-for distance; taunted;
Dissentient and disquiet guest, the soul.

II

Would I were done with flesh, or flesh with me,
—Frailty from frailty seeking prop and stay!—
Would that from all such trammels I were free,
Hindered no more by quagmires of the clay,

Then with an energy controlled and fierce
Might I on greater secrets turn, and fight
Through with unswathed and polished weapon; pierce
Through to some wisdom, to some lake of light.

A sinewy spirit, muscular and lean,
Should be my captain, striding ever on
Over harsh mountains where the wind blew keen,
Peak after peak, till the last peak was won.

Angry I strive, loving the world I hate,
Hating the flesh I love; but all in vain.
Freed for an hour, then, fall'n from ghostly state,
Sink to the clasp of siren foes again.

III

(Yet much is merry in men's moods diverse.
I am no mystic, I, that I should preach
With lips string-drawn as tight as miser's purse,
Dispense thin wisdom by my scrannel speech;

No, none, thank God, can more have loved good laughter,
Beauty, well-being, perilous lottery,
Or paid the reckoning that followed after
With smaller grudge to justice than did I.)

IV

Sometimes I met with one, and would have cried,
"Pilgrim! by the proud manner of your going
Clearly you ask no alms when ills betide.
Though of your journey's end I have no knowing,
Travel a little distance by my side.
Lonely am I; lonely; I have not spoken
Closely with friend this many a questing day;
Body, my beast of burden, stumbles broken,
Rowelled by desperate spur along the way.
Pilgrim, if lonely spirit cross another
And pride in me salute in you your pride,
Shall we not either recognise a brother?"

But reticence held me, and I passed him wide.

V

And sometimes met with those who offered me
Comfort upholstered like a harlot's bed
With winks for ribbons, shrugs to swansdown wed,
And squalor under frowsy frippery.

This draggletail of passion should be mine,
This slattern bastard born of spleen and lust,

Convention's shrewd Bacchante, if I must
Yield to the senses' feverish anodyne!

But I would turn, and, half-defeated, failing,
(How near defeat, they never guessed or knew,)
Load my last breath with scorn, and cry "You? *You?*"
And cry, at bay before their vanguard, railing,

VI

"What! *you* had vision? mountains, comets, seas,
Wild storm, wild beauty, wild embattled flames,
You harnessed to your tongues with hackneyed ease.
Tamers of splendour! those familiar names

Troubled you not, less kingly, more remote
Than gain and ease, your god, your man-made grail.
Not nature's giants, not cosmic menace smote
Your souls with awe, or thrust you down the scale.

No, nor the thoughts your thoughts could not embrace,
A God's intention, void, sublime, or strange,
The birth or death of time, the bourn of space,
Nor unimaginable colours' range,

Nor the continuous eastward roll of earth,
Half, in the energy of day aware;
Half, where the sweeping shadow curves its girth,
Within night's darkened temple cowled in prayer.

No deep misgivings, no mysterious faith;
Your very god was passed from hand to hand;
You had no inkling of the nobler breath
Blown on the spark you could not understand.

VII

"The little spark within the heart of man.
  How should you know the desperate clutch of fingers
  That feel the moment slipping, feel the dear
  Infrequent moment slipping as it lingers,

The flaming hour ironic in its fleetness,
  The rush of vision swift beyond belief?
  Near, as the dead to the incredulous living;
  So dead, the heart is rigid with its grief.

What would you offer me as compensation
  After your sloth had blanketed my fire?
  Your deepest peace, satiety Lethean;
  Your aim, diversion; and your spur, desire.

Tragic, or merry, be the body's passion,
  Ordained or gay; not, not the sordid mean!
  Your soul's a skinny waif, that was not driven
  To sin, but sought small solaces unclean.

You struck no fire from flint; you neither knew
  Fasting nor feasting; vigour, nor a kiss;
  The silk pavilioned bed of Aphrodite,
  Or woodland hardihood of Artemis.

VIII

"Ashamed of tolerance, but more ashamed
  Of hot intolerance; who hold the snare
  Less perilous when fraudulently named;
  Forgetting folly, while remembering care;

Who shun the sinner with averted eyes;
  Mistrust the impulse, danger in its breath;
  Who think truth wholly truth, lies wholly lies;
  Who never lived, but duly wept at death;

Who could not gaily stake the cherished whole
Upon the spinning coin's fantastic turn;
Who count the moneyed value of your soul,
And give, but, giving, claim the just return.

IX

"I'll dip contempt's broad ladle for a measure
Lest I accept reprieve in such a guise,
Such cheap attainment where I most despise,
Or lull disquiet by such sham of pleasure.

Love, amongst counterfeits and marsh-light gleams
Already arch-impostor, doubly aped
By lust, to parody (most rarely shaped),
The consummation of our difficult dreams!"

HOME

NIGHT

To H. G. N.

Moonlight through lattice throws a chequered square;
Night! and I wake in my low-ceilinged room
To lovely silence deep with harmony;
Sweet are the flutes of night-time, sweet the spell
Lies between day and day. This wise old night,
That, unreproachful, gives the pause to strife!
The murmurous diapason of the dark
Within the house made quick and intimate
By tiny noise—a bat? a mouse? a moth
Bruising against the ceiling? or a bird
Nested beneath the eaves? night, grave and huge
Outside with swell of sighing through the boughs,
Whispering far over unscythèd meadows,
Dying in dim cool cloisters of the woods.

I have been absent. I have found unchanged
The oaks, the slope and order of the fields;
I knew the wealden fragrance, and that old
Dear stubborn enemy of mine, the clay.
Nothing to mark the difference of year
But young wheat springing where I left the roots,
And last year's pasture browned to this year's plough;
Last year the crop was niggard on the orchard,
But blossom now foretells the weighted branches,
And the great stack, that like a galleon
Rode beneath furled tarpaulins last July,
Showed its bare brushwood as I passed today.
Where the sun rises, that I know of old;
Knowledge precedes me round the turn of the lane,
And I could take you where the orchids grow
Friendly with cowslips; where the bluebell pulls
Smooth from its bulb, bleached where it grew concealed,
Hidden from light; the tiny brook is eager,

Quick with spring rains, bright April rains, and fills
The pool where drowsy cattle slouch to drink.

Familiar! oh, familiar! native speech
Comes not more readily than that dear sense
Of bend and depth of country. This is Kent,
Unflaunting England, where the steaming mould,
Not plaintive, not regretful, lies content
That leaves should spring from sacrifice of leaves.

My Saxon weald! my cool and candid weald!
Dear God! the heart, the very heart of me
That plays and strays, a truant in strange lands,
Always returns and finds its inward peace,
Its swing of truth, its measure of restraint,
Here among meadows, orchards, lanes, and shaws.
Take me then close, O branches, take me close;
Whisper me all the secrets of the sap,
You branches fragile, tentative, that stretch
Your moonlit blossom to my open window,
Messengers of the gentle weald, encroaching
So shyly on the shelter of the house;
Cradle me, hammock me amongst you; let
Night's quietude so drench my sleepy spirit
That morning shall not rob me of that calm.
Your buds against my pulses; so I lie
Wakeful as though in tree-tops, and the sap
Creeps through my blood, up from the scented earth.

. . . The birds are restless underneath the eaves,
Down in the byre the uneasy cattle stir,
And through the fret of branches grows the dawn.

V. SACKVILLE-WEST

A Saxon Song

Tools with the comely names,
Mattock and scythe and spade,
Couth and bitter as flames,
Clean, and bowed in the blade,—
A man and his tools make a man and his trade.

Breadth of the English shires,
Hummock and kame and mead,
Tang of the reeking byres,
Land of the English breed,—
A man and his land make a man and his creed.

Leisurely flocks and herds,
Cool-eyed cattle that come
Mildly to wonted words,
Swine that in orchards roam,—
A man and his beasts make a man and his home.

Children sturdy and flaxen
Shouting in brotherly strife,
Like the land they are Saxon,
Sons of a man and his wife,—
For a man and his loves make a man and his life.

From a Diary, January 1918

Joy have I had of life this vigorous day
Since sunrise when I took the wealden way,
And my fair country as I rapid strode
Lay round the turn of the familiar road
In mists diaphanous as seas in foam.

And all the orchards cried me welcome home.

I drove the spade that turned the heavy loam,
Bending the winter to the needs of spring,
    The soft air winnowing
The thistledown that blew along the hedge.
A little moorhen rippled in the sedge;
A distant sheep-dog barked; the day was still,
For summer's ghost in winter lay upon the hill.
I worked in peace; an aeroplane above
Crooned through the heaven coloured like a dove.

    Within the house I lit a fire
And coaxed the friendly kettle on to boil.
My boots were heavy with the wealden soil,
My hunger eager from the glow of toil.
Fresh bread had I; brown eggs; a little meat;
Clear water, and an apple sweet.
Freedom I drank for my delirious wine,
And Shelley gave me company divine.
    What more could heart desire?

And when the orange of the sunset burned,
I laid aside my tools and townward turned,
Seeing across the uplands of the Weald
The ploughteams straining on the half-brown field.
I sang aloud; my limbs were rich with health,
As brooding winter rich with summer's wealth.

BEECHWOODS AT KNOLE

How do I love you, beech trees, in the autumn,
Your stone-grey columns a cathedral nave
Processional above the earth's brown glory!

I was a child, and loved the knurly tangle
Of roots that coiled above a scarp like serpents,
Where I might hide my treasure with the squirrels.

I was a child, and splashed my way in laughter
Through drifts of leaves, where underfoot the beechnuts
Split with crisp crackle to my great rejoicing.

Red are the wooded slopes below Shock Tavern,
Red is the bracken on the sandy Furze-field,
Red are the herds of deer by Bo-Pit Meadows,

The tawny deer that nightly through the beechwoods
Roar out their challenge, carrying their antlers
Proudly beneath the antlered moonlit branches.

I was a child, and heard the red deer's challenge
Prowling and baying underneath my window,
Never a cry so haughty or so mournful.

Leopards at Knole

Leopards on the gable-ends,
Leopards on the painted stair,
Stiff the blazoned shield they bear,
Or and gules, a bend of vair,
Leopards on the gable-ends,
     Leopards everywhere.

Guard and vigil in the night
While the ancient house is sleeping
They three hundred years are keeping,
Nightly from their stations leaping,
Shadows black in moonlight bright,
     Roof to gable creeping.

Rigid when the day returns,
Up aloft in sun or rain
Leopards at their posts again
Watch the shifting pageant's train;
And their jewelled colour burns
     In the window-pane.

Often on the painted stair,
As I passed abstractedly,
Velvet footsteps, two and three,
Padded gravely after me.
—There was nothing, nothing there,
     Nothing there to see.

April

When evening sun had beat the rain
And skies were washed so primrose-clean,
We swung the orchard gate again
To let the cattle down the lane;

To let with ripened udders pass
The heavy milch-cows one by one,
And underfoot the blossom was
Like scattered snow upon the grass.

The steep wet road was like a shield
After the rain; and, slouching on,
We idly grumbled at the yield
Of apple-orchards in the Weald.

Arcady in England

I met some children in a wood,
A happy and tumultuous rout
That came with many a wanton shout
And darted hither and about
(As in a stream the fickle trout),
To ease their pagan lustihood.

And in their midst they led along
A goat with wreaths about his neck
That they had taken pains to deck
To join the bacchanalian throng.

And one of them was garlanded
With strands of wild convolvulus
About his ringlets riotous,
And carried rowan-berries red.

And one, the eldest of the band,
Whose life was seven summers glad,
Was all in flowered muslin clad,
And naked dancing feet she had
To lead the sylvan saraband.
With hazel skin and coral bead
A gipsy dryad of the mead
She seemed; she led the gay stampede
With fruited branches in her hand.

For all were bearing autumn fruit;
Some, apples on the loaded bough,
And pears that on the orchard's brow
With damask-plums are hanging now;
And much they had of woodland loot,
Of berries black and berries blue,
Of fircones, and of medlars too;
And one, who bore no plunder, blew
On reeds like an Arcadian flute.

They passed, and still I stood knee-deep
In thymy grass to watch their train.
They wound along the wooded lane
And crossed a streamlet with a leap,
And as I saw them once again
They passed a shepherd and his sheep.

And you might think, I made this song
For joy of song as I strode along
One day between the Kentish shaws,
Slashing at scarlet hips and haws.
But thinking so, you nothing know
Of children taken unawares,
Of tinkers' tents among the gorse,
The poor lean goat, the hobbled horse,
And painted vans for country fairs.

Testament

When I am dead, let not my limbs be given
To rot amongst the dead I never knew,
But cast my ashes wide under wide heaven,
Or to my garden let me still be true,

And, like the ashes I was wont to save
Preciously from the hearth beneath my fire,
Lighten the soil with mine. Not, not the grave!
I loved the soil I fought, and this is my desire.

Sonnet

This little space which scented box encloses
Is blue with lupins and is sweet with thyme.
My garden all is overblown with roses,
My spirit all is overblown with rhyme,
And like a drunken honeybee I waver
From house to garden and again to house,
And, undetermined which delight to favour,
On verse and rose alternately carouse.

Adam, were you, in your primeval plenty,
A poet and a gardener in one?
Did you with easy songs the blossoms sheave,
In Eden where the blooms by ten and twenty
Sprang up beneath the magic of the sun,
To deck the brows of your capricious Eve?

Full Moon

She was wearing the coral taffeta trousers
Someone had brought her from Ispahan,
And the little gold coat with pomegranate blossoms,
And the coral-hafted feather fan;
But she ran down a Kentish lane in the moonlight,
And skipped in the pool of the moon as she ran.

She cared not a rap for all the big planets,
For Betelgeuse or Aldebaran,
And all the big planets cared nothing for her,
That small impertinent charlatan;
But she climbed on a Kentish stile in the moonlight,
And laughed at the sky through the sticks of her fan.

AD ASTRA

AD ASTRA

I

Conqueror! what have you seen in the heavens?
Star-dust is in your hair.
Say, have you woken the sleeping thunder
And taken it unaware?
Come on the storm as a wild beast crouching,
And mocked at it in its lair?

Ridden the wind as a riotous charger,
Your hand in his mane entwined,
As a new unbroken Pegasus,
That a master had divined?
A boast for a man to bring down from heaven,
"I have bridled the wild East wind!"

Gazed in the mirror of unshed dew-ponds,
Bathed in the rivers of rain?
Caught at the meteor's sparks in passing,
And flung them to earth for grain?
Dropped in the wake of the scattered handfuls
To the morning earth again?

How have you raced with the car of Apollo,
A trial of strength indeed,
He in his golden chariot standing
And lashing his golden steed,
You with your glimmering wings of silver
And unconquerable speed?

What of the sirens that dwell in the heavens
In a palace of cloud and air?
As a lover of nymphs inviolate,
Of sirens with rainbow hair,
Have you dwelt like a new Odysseus
With the sirens of the air?

Speak! have you guarded Diana's uprising
From a couch of mist and sheen?
Speak! have you watched Diana's disrobing
After her reign as queen?
Speak! for your eyes are eloquent
With the mysteries they have seen.

And your feet, which have trod in unlaboured fields,
Are with wingèd sandals shod,
And the hawthorn stick at the touch of your hand
Has turned to a wingèd rod,
And your eyes and lips are burnished gold
With the kiss of the bright sun-god.

II

Son of the morning, son of the daybreak,
Son of the stars and sky,
Son of the clean untrodden places,
Son of the air am I

I am the sailor of the heavens,
And the Viking of the gale,
The cloud-built galleon is my vessel,
And the bellying cloud my sail.

I am the reaper of the heavens,
With the sickle moon in my hand.
I am the minstrel of the heavens,
With the birds that rise from land.

I am the hunter of the heavens,
With the night-hounds for my pack,
Lord of unbroken solitudes
That I am the first to track.

Son of the tempest, son of the moonlight,
Son of the silver sky,
Son of the clean untrodden places,
Son of the air am I

FROM "A MASQUE OF YOUTH"

A MOCK-HEROIC POEM

From "A Masque of Youth"

(The scene is laid in a circular space of grass in a garden, enclosed by a stone balustrade broken at intervals by statues of sylvan deities. A background of cypresses. An assembly of dim figures.

Right, the Muse of Tragedy *upon a raised throne. Centre, a great convoluted shell, in which a naked youth lies sleeping.)*

Melpomene: *(She is crowned with vine-leaves, shod with the cothurnus, and carries in her hand a tragic mask)*

O population beautiful and strange
Haunting the curtained boundaries of youth,
Children among immortals, swift of range,
Light-footed, gay of glance, evasive, shy,
Truth robed in fantasy, truth in untruth
That all men apprehend and most pass by,
—You that come crowding and inquisitive
With covert laugh, quick hands, and eyes that live,
Wingèd and whispering and fugitive,
Wide generosities and proud beliefs,
Flamboyant hopes and lovely rainbow griefs,
Rare reverence, lusty audacity,
Faith with bound eyes, arrogant certainty,
Slim fancy with her finger to her lips,
Bright-haired adventure, mother of all ships,
Pale wanton nymphs, quarry of men and gods,

She addresses the assembly.

And dappled centaurs from the dappled woods,—
Draw near.—Here lies, that all may see him well,
A naked Youth within a conchèd shell,
Asleep, in nudity most beautiful.
His arm is flung beneath his lovely head,
He sleeps as sound as in his mortal bed;
Yet him the dolphins hither bore
And all the waters founted with their spouting,
The river-horses galloped by the shore,

She addresses the assembly.

And little wine-drunk sons of love ran shouting,
But he lies victim to the poppy-bell.

Now set I forth in briefest argument
The causes of our present tournament,
Saying how tender Grief and laughing Joy
Strove for possession of the mortal boy,
—As once upon the traveller of old
The sun shone warmly and the wind blew cold,—
And ages long endured their pleasant strife
Renewed with each young adolescent life,
And neither triumphed, for in early years
Youth freely gave to Grief his secret tears
(Grief for grief's sake, which youth to Youth endears),
And sorrows of his melancholy heart,
And Joy, her garlands drooping, stood apart;
Till Love drew near to play his part.

She tells the occasion
of the masque.

Ah! then forgotten were the mournful days.
Youth crowned his head with flowers and
    with bays;
He flung the leopard-skin about his loins,
And bracelets jangled at his wrists like coins,
Nor was the triumph of his singing mute
When at his lips the windy flute
Mingled its treble with the chords of praise
And melody hung scented round his ways.
Proud in his beauty and his sinews' girth
He strode in strength and conquest on the earth,
Or measured down the terraced olive-groves
Intrepid footsteps with the centaur's hooves.
The pleasant valleys echoed with his mirth,
And in the morning resonant and still
His voice was heard like music on the hill.

She tells of Youth
in Love.

So ever ran the course of youth the same,
And Joy and Grief strove on; Grief could not claim
That Love had played unfairly in the game
Since often some poor weeping love-lorn child

Returned to her with sorrow wild,
And cast his broken flute upon the ground
And all his ornaments with tears defiled.

Now Joy this pretty mortal boy has found
And brought him hither, that by our consent
The rivals try their strength, and one be crowned.
Conditional thereon, that Love be bound
To take no action in the tournament.

*   *   *   *   *

1st Spirit: How richly stirs his craving blood
   tonight
   For songs of freedom all among the stars!
   Thoughts like a flock of birds in summer light
   Circle beyond the reach of lifted arms,
   And deeds beyond the scope of life's alarms
      Float into sight,
   And pass, yet undefined, through heaven's bars.

They press forward round the shell.

2nd Spirit: It is the hour of twilight, still, profound,
   When dreams and visions in their legions fly
   On fancy's horses mounted, robed and crowned
   With streaming flames, an aureole of fire,
   And pass, the eagle shapes of man's desire,
      Towards the sunset bound,
   In wingèd ride across the evening sky.
3rd Spirit: He stirs disquieted, he stirs again.
   The stamping hoofs of that proud galaxy
   In passing struck from space the spangled rain
   And flung the ardent fragments down to him
   That scorched his mortal soul through vision dim.
      O shackled soul in pain
   Tortured by glimpses of divinity!
2nd Spirit: What shall we sing in praise of youth? the free,
   The clarion years, the redolent years of youth?
   Youth that loved gold and scarlet pageantry
   And caught the fringe upon the robe of truth?

1st Spirit: Gay youth, that goes, with some familiar friend,
　　On quest of hopes heroic, quest of shores
　　Untravelled, with the heart of conquerors,
　　Eager and brave, and talking without end
　　Of high, magnificent, and cleanly things
　　Rich as the sunset, swift as cormorants' wings
　　That sweep the waters,—youth, whose destiny
　　Sails like a ship upon a virgin sea.
2nd Spirit: Whose heart is as a glowing forge at night
　　Wherein the blacksmith, gleaming with his sweat
　　Like some gigantic negro in the light
　　Of angry fires that touch his limbs of jet,
　　Strikes at the clanging anvil of his thought.
3rd Spirit: Sing to him, sing! till he be so distraught,
　　So drunken and enraptured,
　　That all his heart be captured.
Folly (to Adventure): Gipsy, what have you in your pack
　　Bound with old thongs across your back?
　　Poplin, dimity, huckaback,
　　　　Who draws the prize?

　　Tumble your treasures out on the grass:
　　A wine-dark ruby, a shine of brass,
　　Aladdin's lamp, and a magic glass,
　　　　And a last surprise.

　　Dip in your hands, you wayward crew,
　　The peddler caters for all of you;
　　You press, like a crowd of girls, anew,
　　　　With your eager eyes;
　　Dip in your hands, there are treasures free,
　　Curious pearls, and chalcedony,
　　And the cap of invisibility,
　　But the thing you will none of you ever see
　　　　Is the last surprise.
Imagination: I am the swift omnipotent magician;
　　All bounty's in my gift, all songs unsung,
　　All slumbering chords, all undiscovered crafts
　　Baffling their premature interpreters;

No law's beyond my searching; I'll condemn
No vice, despise no sorrow, scorn no joy,
Deride no virtue, throw no stone at Pilate,
But sweep my mantle round humanity
And round the pomp of nature; naught I'll find
Too mean, too great, too little, or too spacious;
Mine be the secrets both of hearts and stars,
(Small, measureless hearts; great, measurable stars;)
And love's old barbarous reiteration
I'll tolerate, and the great self-less peace
Like the deep sea's perpetual repose.

I'll not be parsimonious of my wealth.
I'll fill your heaven with many coloured moons
And hang such variable tides upon them
As strew the astonished fish along the shores.
I'll bring the planets nearer: I'll attract
Saturn within his hoop of shining rings;
I'll summon a great conclave of the comets
Which hitherto were strangers to each other,
And man, at nightfall standing on the crest
Of a familiar hill, shall marvelling stare
Into an unfamiliar firmament.
I'll show you Jupiter's rebel satellite
That on the outer fringe of measured space
Backwards revolves, striving against the law
That chains her anger to an irksome orbit.

I'll dry the seas and bring the unknown lands
To light, that on unchristened continents
Man stray dry-foot from Africa to Asia.
Oh, what new rivers then, what deep, deep lakes,
What caverns and what cliffs, what strange ravines,
What deserts, what denuded leagues of plain,
Should offer to his swarming multitude!
Peaks shall be islands, islands shall be peaks,
When I reverse the ordering and make
A mountainous Pacific continent,
A Himalayan archipelago.

And all the daily and the lovely things,
—The fawn's late bed of bracken, newly warmed,
The nets of fishermen through water sinking,
Drawn up all hoar with flake of silver scales
And round clear drops that tremble from the mesh,—
These little things, these nimble shy delights,
With the quick magic of significance
I'll not despise to startle into being.

SONGS OF FANCY

Songs of Fancy: I

Your caravel was loosely moored,
—So lightly moored, so slightly moored,—
It ranged with every passing swell,
Your gipsy-hearted caravel
That only silken ropes secured.

I dreamt that you might slip away,
—Might slide away, might glide away,—
When I was absent, on a breeze
Enticing you to other seas
With whispers of a lovelier day.

The sirens underneath the stars,
—The flaunting stars, the haunting stars,—
Would cast adrift your mooring-rope
(Farewell, my heart! farewell, my hope!)
And stretch the sails upon your spars,

And you would sail before the wind,
—Elusive wind, delusive wind,—
All radiant on your moonlit deck,
And not a moment would you reck
Of me whom you had left behind.

You'd come to legendary coasts,
To nameless coasts, to tameless coasts,
And hear of unimagined things:
The exploits of vainglorious kings,
Their fabled pride, and braggart boasts;

Iris you'd meet, and Mercury,
Sweet Mercury, fleet Mercury;
You'd see the constellations change,
You'd pass the magnet mountain-range
That draws a ship to mystery;

You'd see, on black basaltic rocks,
On jaggèd rocks, on craggèd rocks,
The lonely Polyphemus stand,
The scourge and terror of the land,
Amongst his decimated flocks.

You'd turn from thence; a rainbow arc,
A magic arc, a tragic arc,
That spanned the sky from east to west
Might lure you on a dreamer's quest
And close for ever on your barque.

Ah God! perhaps this very night,
This hated night, this fated night,
You heard the breeze, the sirens' spell. . .
I faint, I look; your caravel
In harbour still lies gold and white.

Sing of enchanted palaces
In Tripoli, in Tripoli,
Above the sighing and the surge
Of the moaning sea, of the slothful sea;
Of palaces upon the verge
Of the sleepy sea, of the sleepy sea.

Sing of enchanted palaces
In Venice by the broad lagoons
Of long ago, of long ago,
Where cupolas like cuspèd moons
In waters dim reflected glow,
And ghosts of stately frigatoons
In dusky waters come and go.

Sing of enchanted palaces
In cities set by gilded seas,
Slenderly mimicked in the waves
The lace of spires and balconies,
The oriels and the architraves,
—Dreams! dreams! where lead such dreams as these?

Songs of Fancy: III

Was it but a random bird,
Harlequin on breast and wing?
Or through aspens whispering
Was it some rare flute you heard,
That you followed, wandering?

Followed all that onward fled,
Hares and squirrels, bounding roes,
All that through the woodland goes,
Wind that murmurs overhead,
Leaves that scamper, stream that flows.

Straight the pathway you forsook
Tempted by the beckoning
Of the winded poplar's swing,
Tempted by the onward brook,
In pursuit adventuring,

By the bluebell's fleeting drift,
By the splash of light and shade
Down the ride in patterns laid,
By the distant sunshine rift,
Promise of the open glade.

There, where they had seen you go,
Those who loved you called your name,
Searching, seeking, to and fro.
True, to answer them you came,
But your eyes were not the same.

SWEET TIME

Sweet Thyme, that underfoot so meekly grows
In humble company
Of splendid rose,
Is all content to be
The acolyte, as each man knows,
Of lavender, of rue, and rosemary.

Sweet Time, that pilfers all my precious years,
Will no wise blandishment
Or threat of tears
Bring you to pause, content?
—Hard-hearted greybeard, as he went,
He winked at me, and clicked his wicked shears.

A Cypress Avenue

Like hooded monks they go,
    Two by two,
Pointed and black and slow,
    Chanting for you,
Chanting without a tear,
    A final song,
Chanting above your bier
    Passing along,
Far from the living sun,
    Far from the day,
—My lover, let us run
    Away, away!

Mirage

There travelled north from Kurdistan along the lone Siberian trails
A merchant with his caravan and Eastern barter in his bales.
He rode ahead, he rode apart, the city of Irkutsk his goal,
Upon his lean Circassian foal, and after came the lumbering cart
With creaking wheel, deliberate spoke, and water-bullocks in the yoke;
And after these in single string the boorish camels following,
Slouching with high unwieldy packs like howdahs piled upon their
    backs;
With slaver hanging from their lips and hatred worming in their brain
They slouched beneath their drivers' whips across the white and
    mournful plain.

The merchant riding on alone saw not the white incessant snow,
He only saw the metal's glow, the colour of the precious stone;
He lingered on the merchandise that he had brought from Kurdistan,
And turned, and swept his caravan with doting and voluptuous eyes,
For there were choice Bokhara rugs, and daggers with Damascus blade
And hafts of turquoise-studded jade, and phials rich with scented
    drugs,
Koràns inscribed on ass's skin, and bales of silk from Temesvàr,
And silver ear-rings beaten thin, and bargains from the cool bazaar.

He felt the gold already pouched, he crooned to it with horrid love,
As still the camels onward slouched with hatred of the men that drove.

For thirty days the caravan trailed on behind the merchant's foal,
Through Persia and through Turkestan, the city of Irkutsk their goal;
They passed the fruitful hill-girt lands where dwelt the fair-skinned
    Grecian race,
And came into the wilder place, and sighted vagrant Cossack bands
That wandered with their flocks and herds, and trafficked with the
    train of Kurds;
They stirred the ghost of Tamerlane, who swept that way with Tartar
    hordes,
The ghosts of dead barbarian lords, the Asiatic hurricane;

They crossed the mighty road that runs from Moscow through to
    China's wall,
And trod the path of nomad Huns and knew Siberia's white pall
When fields of Persian asphodel were visions of a distant day
And boundless snow around them lay, and noiseless snow for ever fell,
Where soon the fleeting day was done, and on the hard horizon low
They saw the scarlet ball of sun divided by the ridge of snow
Sink down in skies incarnadine; and still with their disjointed gait
And nursing their malignant hate, the camels kept unbroken line.

When yet a hundred miles or more stretched out between them and
    their goal
The merchant riding on before drew rein on his Circassian foal
And called a halt with lifted hand as he had done unfailingly
Each night since the monotony began with that unvaried land.
The dusk was suddenly alive as shouting voices passed the word,
And all the drowsy train was stirred with movement like a shaken hive.
The master merchant stiff from cramp was calling for his saddle flask,
As each to his accustomed task ran swiftly in the growing camp.
A tent like an inverted bell, all scarlet with the dyes of Tyre,
Was lifted rapidly and well, and like a torch the kindled fire
Destroyed the night with leaping tongue, and in a circle round the
    glow
Men shovelled back the melting snow, and skins and Khelim rugs
    were flung—
And unforgotten were the needs of water-bullocks standing by
Whose brows are stained with orange dye, whose horns are looped
    with turquoise beads.
The pariah dogs that slink and prowl secured their meat with furtive
    growl,
And one by one the camels bent complaining to their warty knees
And grumbled at the men that went to loose their girths and give
    them ease.

The merchant brooded silently on avaricious visions bright
And listened to the revelry his men were making in the night.
For one, a young and favourite Kurd, a mongrel child of the bazaar,
Whose voice was like a singing bird, was striking on a harsh guitar—

I know a Room where tulips tall
    And almond-blossom pale
Are coloured on the frescoed wall.

I know a River where the ships
    Drift by with ghostly sail
And dead men chant with merry lips.

I know the Garden by the sea
    Where birds with painted wings
Mottle the dark magnolia Tree.

I know the never-failing Source,
    I know the Bush that sings,
The Vale of Gems, the flying Horse.

I know the Dog that was a Prince,
    The talking Nightingale,
The Hill of glass, the magic Quince.

I know the lovely Lake of Van;
    Yet, knowing all these things,
       I wander with a Caravan,
       I wander with a Caravan!

The cold moon rose remotely higher, insensibly the voices hushed,
And men with wine and laughter flushed were sleeping all around the
    fire,
Till one alone sat on erect, his ready gun across his knees,
The sentry of the night elect, guardian of sleeping destinies.
The water-bullocks lay as dead; the dogs drew near with noiseless
    tread,
And huddled in a loose-limbed heap beside the fire, and through their
    sleep
They twitched at some remembered hunt; the merchant in his
    sheepskin rolled
Within the tent saw dreams of gold; the camels with uneasy grunt
And quake of their distorted backs slept on with loathing by their
    packs.

At dawn the weary sentry rose to throw some brushwood on the
    flames,
Called on his comrades by their names, and turned to greet the
    endless snows,
But then from his astonished lips a cry of unbelieving rang
And all the men towards him sprang, the camel drivers with their
    whips,
The bullock driver with his yoke, and gazed in loud bewilderment
Till slowly in his fur-lined cloak the merchant issued from his tent.
Then he too started at the sight and clamoured with his clamorous
    men,
And swore he could not see aright, and rubbed his eyes and stared
    again;
The camels came with lurching tread and stood in loose fantastic ring
With necks outstretched and swaying head and mouths all slackly
    slobbering,
And drew from some unclean recess within their body's secret lair
A bladder smeared with filthiness that bubbled on the morning air.

For there upon the shining plain a city radiantly lay,
All coloured in the rising day, amid the snow a jewelled stain,
And in her walls a spacious gate gave entrance to a varied stream
Of folk that went incorporate like figures in a silent dream,
And high above the roofs arose, more coloured for the hueless snows,
The domes of churches, bronze and green, like peacocks in their
    painted sheen.

The merchant, with a trembling hand extended far, extended wide
Against illusion's fairyland, at length articulately cried:
"Irkutsk! but twice a hundred miles remained of weary pilgrimage
Before we hoped with happy smiles to reach our final anchorage.

But look again. That rosy tower that rises like a tulip straight
Within the walls beside the gate, a balanced plume, a springing flower,
And pointed with a lance-like spire of bronze, was fifty years ago
—A boy, I saw it standing so,—demolished and destroyed by fire."

And one, a venerable Kurd, took up again the fallen word:
"I travelled both as boy and man between Irkutsk and Kurdistan,

But never since my beard was grown saw I that inn beside the way
Wherewith the Council made away, full fifty counted years aflown."

They gazed upon the marvel long, the spectre city wonderful,
Until the youth who made the song cried out, "We grow too fanciful.
Irkutsk with roofs of coloured tiles lies distant twice a hundred miles,
And this, a city of the shades, a rainbow of the echoing air,
As fair as false, and false as fair, already into nothing fades."

And like a bubble, like the mist that in the valley faintly swirls,
Like orient sheen on sulky pearls, like hills remotely amethyst,
Like colours on Phœnician glass, like plumage on the 'fisher's wing,
Like music on the breath of spring, they saw the vision lift and pass,
Till only white unbroken snow stretched out before the caravan,
And the bewildered heart of man truth from delusion could not know.
But all the long laborious train moved slowly on its course again
Across the snow unbroken, white, and nursing each his private creed,
The merchant his illusive greed, the camels their illusive spite.

CHINOISERIE

(Villanelle) *For B. M.*

Lotus flowers clustering
Round your feet in storeys laid,
Splendid daughter of a King.

In a graven vase of Ming
Peaches, apricots of jade,
Lotus flowers clustering,

All their scentless riches bring,
All around your throne displayed,
Costly daughter of a King.

What young prince astonishing
Rides along the inky glade,
Lotus flowers clustering

Round his camel travelling?
See the leopards unafraid,
Slender daughter of a King!

Coromandel picturing,
Strangely, marvellously made.
Lotus flowers clustering,

Nightingales that cannot sing,
What celestial escapade
Are they nightly witnessing,
Through lotus flowers clustering,
O subtle daughter of a King?

Colour

In the last orgy of Creation's hour,
—That fabled day, when all to sudden birth
Sprang,—as the toy of his redundant mirth
God tossed in bounty Colour to the earth.
He held the exquisite and pallid flower,
Spoke new strange words, and in his hands there blushed
The great white rose to crimson slowly flushed.

SAILING

Sailing Ships

Lying on Downs above the wrinkling bay
I with the kestrels shared the cleanly day,
The candid day; wind-shaven, brindled turf;
Tall cliffs; and long sea-line of marbled surf
From Cornish Lizard to the Kentish Nore
Lipping the bulwarks of the English shore,
While many a lovely ship below sailed by
On unknown errand, kempt and leisurely;
And after each, oh, after each, my heart
Fled forth, as, watching from the Downs apart,
I shared with ships good joys and fortunes wide
That might befall their beauty and their pride;

Shared first with them the blessèd void repose
Of oily days at sea, when only rose
The porpoise's slow wheel to break the sheen
Of satin water indolently green,
When for'ard the crew, caps tilted over eyes,
Lay heaped on deck; slept; murmured; smoked; threw dice;
The sleepy summer days; the summer nights
(The coast pricked out with rings of harbour-lights),
The motionless nights, the vaulted nights of June
When high in the cordage drifts the entangled moon,
And blocks go knocking, and the sheets go slapping,
And lazy swells against the sides come lapping;
And summer mornings off red Devon rocks,
Faint inland bells at dawn and crowing cocks.

Shared swifter days, when headlands into ken
Trod grandly; threatened; and were lost again,
Old fangs along the battlemented coast;
And followed still my ship, when winds were most
Night-purified, and, lying steeply over,
She fled the wind as flees a girl her lover,
Quickened by that pursuit for which she fretted,
Her temper by the contest proved and whetted;

Wild stars swept overhead; her lofty spars
Reared to a ragged heaven sown with stars
As leaping out from narrow English ease
She faced the roll of long Atlantic seas;

Her captain then was I, I was her crew,
The mind that laid her course, the wake she drew,
The waves that rose against her bows, the gales,—
Nay, I was more: I was her very sails
Rounded before the wind, her eager keel,
Her straining mast-heads, her responsive wheel,
Her pennon stiffened like a swallow's wing;
Yes, I was all her slope and speed and swing,
Whether by yellow lemons and blue sea
She dawdled through the isles off Thessaly,
Or saw the palms like sheaves of scimitars
On desert's verge below the sunset bars,
Or passed the girdle of the planet where
The Southern Cross looks over to the Bear,
And strayed, cool Northerner beneath strange skies,
Flouting the lure of tropic estuaries,
Down that long coast, and saw Magellan's Clouds arise.

And some that beat up Channel homeward-bound
I watched, and wondered what they might have found,
What alien ports enriched their teeming hold
With crates of fruit or bars of unwrought gold?
And thought how London clerks with paper-clips
Had filed the bills of lading of those ships,
Clerks that had never seen the embattled sea,
But wrote down jettison and barratry,
Perils, Adventures, and the Act of God,
Having no vision of such wrath flung broad;
Wrote down with weary and accustomed pen
The classic dangers of sea-faring men;
And wrote "Restraint of Princes," and "the acts
Of the King's Enemies," as vacant facts,
Blind to the ambushed seas, the encircling roar
Of angry nations foaming into war.

V. SACKVILLE-WEST

PHANTOM

I saw a ship sailing,
No other ship in sight.
Steadily she was sailing
Although the wind fell light.
Although the wind was failing
Still she kept sailing.

No hand there that steered her,
No wind that strained her sheet.
And as I gazed I feared her:
Why should she be so fleet
Since no crew's chanty cheered her,
And no wind neared her?

Her strange sure motion
Carried her swiftly past;
Over the rim of ocean
I watched her dip her mast.
Still no wind blew in motion
Across the ocean.

Genoese Merchants

They garnered wealth from far barbarian shores,
From Caffa, Tyre, and Trebizond,
And Tartar provinces beyond;
Furs, spices, oranges, and slaves.
High galleys waited, runged with tiers of oars,
And rippled their reflection in the waves.

Bearded and serge-clad merchants, tightly-lipped,
They stood in groups along the foreign quays
Watching the cargo shipped
By coloured sons of Asia; these
Groaned loaded up the planks, and rolled
Their burdens down the hold;
And back the planks unburdened nimbly tripped,
Their pumpkin-fluted turbans and their scarves
Ballooning as they swarmed upon the wharves.

And some old shaven brightly-plumaged priest,
Drowsing outside his mosque when shadows fall
Like lengthened lances pointing to the East,
From fourfold minaret,
And through the iron grating in the wall
The sun-flushed Himalaya guards Thibet,
—He, fat and somnolent,
Yawning amongst the pigeons' sleek content,
Opened one crafty, long, Mongolian eye,
And saw the slim Italian passing by
With soft-foot tread
Into the mosque, but never raised his head,
And slipped his cedar beads, and never stirred
Though the quick patter of the coins he heard
Fall in a handful mixed of maize and rice
Flung to the pigeons, coins that were his price.

While far, in Europe, lay the Flemish fairs,
The marts of Ypres, the Jews of busy Thames
Greedy to clutch the unfamiliar gems,
And rummage in the bales of rich exotic wares.

EVENING

When little lights in little ports come out,
Quivering down through water with the stars,
And all the fishing fleet of slender spars
Range at their moorings, veer with tide about;

When race of wind is stilled and sails are furled,
And underneath our single riding-light
The curve of black-ribbed deck gleams palely white,
And slumbrous waters pool a slumbrous world,

—Then, and then only, have I thought how sweet
Old age might sink upon a windy youth,
Quiet beneath the riding-light of truth,
Weathered through storms, and gracious in retreat.

"SUMURUN,"
CORNWALL, 1920

V. SACKVILLE-WEST

A Note About the Author

V. Sackville-West (1892–1952) was an English novelist, poet, journalist, and gardener. Born at Knole, the Sackville's hereditary home in west Kent, Vita was the daughter of English peer Lionel Sackville-West and his cousin Victoria, herself the illegitimate daughter of the 2nd Baron Sackville and a Spanish dancer named Pepita. Educated by governesses as a young girl, Vita later attended school in Mayfair, where she met her future lover Violet Keppel. An only child, she entertained herself by writing novels, plays, and poems in her youth, both in English and French. At the age of eighteen, she made her debut in English society and was courted by powerful and well-connected men. She had affairs with men and women throughout her life, leading an open marriage with diplomat Harold Nicholson. Following their wedding in 1913, the couple moved to Constantinople for one year before returning to settle in England, where they raised two sons. Vita's most productive period of literary output, in which she published such works as *The Land* (1926) and *All Passion Spent* (1931), coincided with her affair with English novelist Virginia Woolf, which lasted from 1925 to 1935. The success of Vita's writing—published through Woolf's Hogarth Press—allowed her lover to publish some of her masterpieces, including *The Waves* (1931) and *Orlando* (1928), the latter being inspired by Sackville-West's family history, androgynous features, and unique personality. Vita died at the age of seventy at Sissinghurst Castle, where she worked with her husband to design one of England's most famous gardens.

A Note from the Publisher

Spanning many genres, from non-fiction essays to literature classics to children's books and lyric poetry, Mint Edition books showcase the master works of our time in a modern new package. The text is freshly typeset, is clean and easy to read, and features a new note about the author in each volume. Many books also include exclusive new introductory material. Every book boasts a striking new cover, which makes it as appropriate for collecting as it is for gift giving. Mint Edition books are only printed when a reader orders them, so natural resources are not wasted. We're proud that our books are never manufactured in excess and exist only in the exact quantity they need to be read and enjoyed.

bookfinity™

Discover more of your favorite classics with Bookfinity™.

- Track your reading with custom book lists.
- Get great book recommendations for your personalized Reader Type.
- Add reviews for your favorite books.
- AND MUCH MORE!

Visit **bookfinity.com** and take the fun Reader Type quiz to get started.

Enjoy our classic and modern companion pairings!

Classic & Modern